ALL ABO[UT]

Margaret Hamilton

Tamra Orr

BLUE
RIVER
PRESS

Indianapolis, Indiana

All About Margaret Hamilton

Copyright © 2023 Blue River Press

Published by Blue River Press
Indianapolis, Indiana
www.brpressbooks.com

Distributed by Cardinal Publishers Group
A Tom Doherty Company, Inc.
www.cardinalpub.com

ISBN: 978-1-68157-136-2
Library of Congress Control Number: 2018943662

Cover Design: David Miles
Original Book Design: Richard Korab, Korab Company Design
Book Design Implementation: Tessa Schmitt
Cover Artist: Nicole McCormick Santiago
Editors: Dani McCormick, Tessa Schmitt
Illustrator: Moriah McReynolds

Printed in the United States of America

10 9 8 7 6 5 4 3 2 1   23 24 25 26 27 28 29 30 31 32

CONTENTS

ALL ABOUT

Margaret Hamilton

When the very first men landed on the Moon on July 20, 1969, more than half a billion people around the world were watching. They were amazed at what they were seeing on their television sets.

As astronaut Neil Armstrong uttered the words, "The Eagle has landed," people erupted with cheers of happiness—and sighs of relief.

The journey to the Moon took years of skill, wisdom, and effort. It involved a huge team of more than 400,000 people — including a young woman named Margaret Hamilton.

Margaret loved numbers from the time she was a child. As an adult, she was fascinated by creating computer software, long before the rest of the world had ever heard of it. After graduating from college in Indiana, Hamilton moved to Massachusetts. She began working on the software that would eventually help create weather forecasts.

Margaret moved from weather to weaponry. Working on computers that took up entire warehouses, she developed software that identified enemy aircraft.

One day she heard that NASA (National

Aeronautics and Space Administration) was looking for computer coders. They wanted to put men on the Moon within a few years. Margaret was thrilled to get the chance to work on something this monumental. At that time, space flight was still an idea that was mostly found in science fiction books and movies.

As time went by, Margaret's value to NASA grew and grew. By the time the Apollo missions were heading for the Moon, Margaret was a valued member on her team. Despite women being in the minority at NASA, she paved the way for future women in STEM (Science, Technology, Engineering, Mathematics).

Over her lifetime, Margaret has received a number of awards in recognition of the work she has done. In November 2016, President Barack Obama gave her the Presidential Medal of Freedom for being a "pioneer in technology."

Margaret's innovative spirit continues to inspire future generations in the STEM industry and beyond. Through her dedication in software engineering, the US has reached new goals once thought to be impossible.

CHAPTER ONE

Asking Questions

One of the earliest lessons Margaret Heafield (later Hamilton) can remember being taught was to ask questions. Both her father and grandfather encouraged her to "keep asking questions until the answers made sense," she recalls. The three of them had many 'what-if' and 'why not' conversations during long car rides.

"These were favorite times, spending time with the two of them," she stated in an online interview. Those talks helped her become curious about the world as a child and adult. Margaret describes her father-daughter relationship as the two of them being "very good friends."

She says that he would listen to her ideas and respond with, "Wow, I never, ever thought of that" and she believed him. Margaret was encouraged

When most children were reading the Wizard of Oz, *Margaret was exploring outside trying to learn about the world.*

to keep questioning because her father always made her feel incredibly smart. "I would just love to get his attention with coming up with these new ideas," she stated. " . . . he would listen to what you had to say. . . and then he'd come up with questions." It encouraged her to stay curious.

Margaret was born on August 17, 1936 in

the small southern Indiana town of Paoli. With just over 2,000 people living there during the 1930s, everyone knew everyone else. Even today, the small city only has a population of roughly 3,700.

Margaret was the Heafield's first child. She was joined two years later by brother David. Sister Kathryn followed in 1941.

Margaret was born in the middle of the Great Depression. During the 1930's, 20,000 schools were closed throughout the country. The economy was in trouble and people had little money to buy things like food and clothes. Paying for school was low on the list of priorities for many, so schools did not receive a lot of funding.

Margaret's mother Ruth Esther Partington was a high school teacher. She graduated from Earlham College in Indiana in 1934.

During her lifetime, she taught at a number of high schools. She often taught home economics, showing students basic life skills such as how to cook and sew. Esther was much-loved by her students.

Margaret's father, Kenneth Heafield, was also

a teacher, as well as a philosopher and poet. He met Esther near the city of Escanaba, Michigan. According to Hamilton, "It was a little town called Garden. It would be lucky if I could say it had 100 people. It was tiny," she continued. Kenneth had a strong belief in the goodness and courage of people.

He wrote many poems. Some were published in a book titled *Beachcomber and Other Poems*. He dedicated the book to Margaret. His poetry often centered on the beauty of nature.

Little information is known about Margaret's childhood other than she did a great deal of moving around. Only a few weeks after she was born, she and her family moved from Paoli, Indiana.

They lived in cities throughout Indiana, Michigan, and Ohio. "It was a lot of little towns that I found myself in for one reason or another," she explained in an interview. "They were usually, as I remember, little towns with the main street that was tiny so you knew all of your neighbors." By the time she was in high school, Margaret's family was living in the Upper Peninsula of Michigan. "I was used to being in classrooms with people I didn't know," explained Margaret, "going to new places and living in different places."

Religion played a big role in the Hamilton household. One of Margaret's grandfathers was a Quaker minister, while the other one was a Protestant minister. In both churches, music was very important. Her grandmother and aunts all played the piano and were quite good at it. Sometimes there were three pianos being played at the same time in her household. "I was not

Margaret is the oldest of all her siblings and cousins. Here, Margaret is pictured with her brother David (far left) and sister Kathryn (far right).

that good at it," admitted Margaret. She loved music but preferred listening to playing. "I loved music of all kinds," she said. Although her family preferred classical music, Margaret enjoyed more popular choices like Elvis or The Doors. "I was sort of rebelling against classical music," she confessed. One of the biggest focuses in Margaret's family was reading and the arts. "We always had books around us and music," she recalled.

Children in the 1940s lived differently than children do now. Mothers were just starting to work outside the home with regularity. Day care centers were starting to become commonplace. Before this, most mothers stayed home with their children while fathers worked.

Because of World War II, there weren't enough men left in the workforce to do the necessary jobs. Many were fighting in Europe or the South Pacific. Who was going to fill the employment gap?

Women rose up to the task, learning how to do the jobs that had been left empty when men became soldiers. They did everything from building cars, planes, and tanks, to growing food for the nation.

The iconic image of Rosie the Riveter became a figurehead that encouraged women to support the war effort by working.

Not everyone supported women joining the workforce though. Many congressmen and child development specialists thought that mothers working out of the home would affect their children. They cautioned mothers to only work if necessary.

When Margaret was growing up, the phrase "latchkey kid" started being used. This described children who let themselves into the house after school, because their mothers were working.

The boys were encouraged to study different subjects in school than the girls. Boys focused on shop class, science, and math, while girls focused on

Rosie the Riveter

Between 1940 and 1950, the number of women in the US workforce rose significantly. The aviation industry saw the largest increase of women in the workforce.

home economics, English, and art.

Margaret later reported to author Dean Robbins that, as a child, she was aware that boys got more opportunities than girls—and she did not like that.

"She made a point of joining the boys' baseball team and even renamed some of the daddy longlegs she found in her yard as 'mommy' longlegs," stated Robbins.

Eventually, the Heafield family moved again, this time to Hancock, Michigan. In 1954, Margaret graduated from Hancock High School. Margaret loved school, although home economics was her least favorite class because "girls were supposed to take it. And, again, it [not taking the class] was rebelling against what we had to do," she recalled.

"I just enjoyed school, but there was just something about math that I enjoyed more than anything else," Margaret stated in a documentary about her life.

Her passion for numbers and math, and her endless curiosity made her a good student. Even when she was quite small, she knew how many miles it was to the Moon (238,855 miles on average).

She used algebra, geometry, and calculus to solve issues she ran into in daily life.

Mr. Philips, Margaret's eleventh grade math teacher, said:

[Margaret] was a very, very talented girl. She was able to comprehend material at a pace that basically no one else I taught was able to do. She had a passion for math. One day, she came to me, and I will never forget this. She asked why doesn't our school have any programs for computer programs? She was just beside herself that this wasn't being offered. Really annoyed. She said to me, 'Math and computer programming are the foundation for progress.' . . . She was right.

During her time in high school, Margaret was very active. She was in choir and band, plus she loved to go horseback riding and play baseball. "You name the hobby, I had that hobby," she stated.

As her years in high school came to an end, it was time to think about college. Margaret knew she wanted to go, but still decided to rebel a little more. She told her father than she had decided not to go attend after all. "He said, 'Fine, that's okay,'" she recalled. "Well, I quickly changed my mind!" She knew she wanted to go—but was still unclear on what degree she wanted to pursue. Should she be a journalist or musician like her grandmothers? Perhaps she would become a teacher like her mother or a philosopher like her father?

She wasn't sure. She had learned a great deal about work she did and did not enjoy from the jobs she held as a teenager. She waited on tables at a resort, worked as a clerk in a drug store, and as a server at a chicken restaurant. For several years, Margaret worked as a guide in an abandoned copper mine. " . . . I started taking people on tours and they started off with like a family a day, two or three people a day," Margaret described. "And then pretty soon it started growing. And I had to start hiring other guides to work for me. And by the end of that year it was like at least 1,000 people a day over the summer." When some of these workers decided to go on strike for more money, it was Margaret who worked to get everyone—including herself—a raise. Within a few years, she was running the overall copper mine! It taught her important life lessons including, as she put it, the concept of "going to work every day and for responsibility and what it means to have responsibility." Those are lessons that she would call on for the rest of her life.

CHAPTER TWO

College in Indiana

It came as little surprise when Margaret decided to attend Earlham College in Richmond, Indiana after she graduated from high school. Earlham was, and still is, a Quaker-based college.

Margaret's grandfather, Eliezer Partingon, had been a Quaker minister. He had taught many of that religion's values to his daughter Esther and his granddaughter Margaret.

Quakers often refer to themselves as "Friends." They believe that all people are created equally and that violence is never the solution. They welcome everyone into their meeting houses.

Earlham College first opened in 1847. It was the second Quaker college in the world at the time. It began accepting non-Quaker students in 1865.

Part of Earlham College's mission statement is to "provide the highest quality undergraduate education...shaped by the distinctive perspectives of the...Quakers."

Today, about 1,200 students attend Earlham, and about ten percent of students identify as Quakers.

Eight members of the Heafield family had already attended Earlham College. Margaret's grandfather had graduated in 1904. Margaret's mother Esther graduated in 1934.

Before enrolling at Earlham, Margaret tried going to the University of Michigan. She planned to get a degree in math and received a good scholarship. However, the university was not the right fit.

"I grew up in tiny little Midwestern towns throughout my childhood, so the University of Michigan seemed too huge and unfriendly," she said in the Winter 2018 issue of Earlham College's magazine *The Earlhamite*. "I'm sure I also had aunts and uncles telling me I should go to Earlham because they had."

So, after leaving the University of Michigan, Margaret considered other institutions and ultimately chose Earlham. She had contemplated attending Stevens College, but it was an all-women's school and that did not appeal to her. It did not feel like a "real world" environment. "I said to my father, 'I don't have anything against women, but it's much more real world like to have everybody in the college, not just say because you're a girl, you're going here or you're a boy so you're going here,'" she explained.

Little is known about Margaret's early years, especially about her years at Earlham. She somehow earned the nickname Bunny, which was a common nickname at the time for women named Bernice or Barbara.

In 1957, she was named the school's Homecoming Queen. She majored in math, as she had planned, but also earned a minor in philosophy, perhaps inspired by her father Kenneth. He told Margaret that he thought math and philosophy had a great deal in common. She graduated in 1958 with a Bachelor of Arts degree, with a plan to become a math professor.

One teacher that truly had an impact on Margaret during her years at Earlham was mathematics Professor Florence Long.

"Math students were like an extended family for her," Margaret told *The Earlhamite*. "She would invite us all to her home and make cucumber sandwiches for us."

Long treated Margaret like family. Margaret found it inspiring. "And I remember thinking, 'I want to do what she's doing,'" she recalled. "I want to teach the kind of mathematics she's teaching. And I want to teach it in college like she's doing."

One more thing happened to Margaret during her years at Earlham College. She met her future husband, James Cox Hamilton. He was Earlham's student body president. James graduated a year after Margaret with a degree in chemistry. He then went to Harvard Law School, where he graduated in 1963.

Because her husband was attending Harvard, Margaret moved to Boston, Massachusetts. She began teaching high school French and math classes

After graduation, James (left) was an active Earlham alum. When he passed away, the college recognized his contributions by establishing the James Cox Hamilton Endowed Scholarship. This scholarship is awarded to students in financial need.

to earn money while James got his law degree.

However, she was not satisfied with this job. She wanted to do and learn more. She had planned to go back to school as soon as James graduated to get an advanced degree in mathematics. She struggled with her current role as James' wife.

"When my husband was in law school, they wanted the law wives, of which I was one, to pour tea," she recalled. "And I said to my husband, 'No way am I pouring tea.'" James was proud of Margaret for taking a stand.

Before any decisions could be made, however, Margaret got an entirely different chance. It took her in directions she could never have imagined.

CHAPTER THREE

From Weather to Weapons

In the 1950s, there was an increased interest in space exploration and growing tension between the United States and the Soviet Union. This pushed people to go to college who hadn't previously considered it, including many women.

"There was a sense of urgency," said Mary Allen Jolley, a legislative aide. She helped draft the National Defense Education Act in 1958 and the Vocational Education Act in 1964. The 1964 act opened up the option of higher education to more people throughout the country.

The ongoing conflict between the Soviet Union and the US grew in a new direction in the late 1950s. On October 4, 1957, a Soviet satellite named *Sputnik* was launched into space.

America's biggest foe had just taken the first step into space exploration. This was not acceptable to the United States. They could not allow the Soviet Union to get ahead of them in science and space exploration. The Space Race had begun.

Sputnik 1 orbited Earth about once every 98 minutes for about three months before it reentered the atmosphere and broke into pieces.

In 1959, Margaret and James became parents when their daughter Lauren was born. Margaret was a wife, mother, and scientist. She kept busy with her family and work. Soon she would find

In 1959, it was common for mothers to quit their jobs and become stay-at-home mothers after having children. Margaret chose to join the fifteen million working women instead.

herself working on a project that would change the world.

Being a mother in the 1950s and 1960s could be difficult, especially when working outside the home. At the time, raising children and house chores were viewed as a woman's responsibility. Without the help of modern technology, this burden grew. Tasks such as washing the dishes or doing laundry was done by hand, taking extra time and effort.

Due to the amount of household work, many women were stay-at-home mothers. For those who worked, no paid maternity leave was offered. Often, women were fired upon becoming pregnant, or suffered a drop in pay. Margaret, was aware of how hard it was to have a child and career, and yet she actively worked to have both.

Margaret's unexpected opportunity came when she applied to work at the Massachusetts Institute of Technology (MIT). Her husband had seen a job opening in the local newspaper and told her about

Massachusetts Institute of Technology (MIT) was established in Cambridge, Massachusetts in 1861. On the 50th anniversary of the Moon Landing, students placed a fake Lunar Module atop the Great Dome (building pictured).

it. It quickly became clear that the Institute wanted her.

MIT had hired its first woman in 1865, making it a very progressive Institute at the time. Margaret Dayton Stinson was hired to manage the chemical supply room. Her job was to keep track of who received what chemicals and when, as well as how much was available.

Shortly after that, in 1870, MIT accepted it's first female student, Ellen Swallow. Since the Institute didn't officially teach women, Swallow was admitted as a "special student" and referred to as the "Swallow Experiment." Although MIT was hesitant to admit Swallow, she soon became a helpful and admired student. After graduating with a bachelor's degree in science, Swallow went on to establish the Women's Laboratory, allowing more women to follow in her footsteps.

In 1882, MIT officially began admitting female students. For the first fifty years of women attending the Institute, female students accounted for only one percent of the student body. However, as men and students joined the war effort during World

Margaret worked in MIT's Lincoln labortories in the early 1960's. She worked with Professor Edward N. Lorenz (left).

War II, women were encouraged to further their education.

Hours after MIT expressed interest in hiring Margaret, she recalls, "[setting] up interviews with two project managers at MIT. Both of them offered me a position on the same day as the interviews. I did not want to hurt anyone's feelings," she explained, "so I told them to flip a coin to decide which group would hire me." The winner was Professor Edward N. Lorenz.

Lorenz's focus was on meteorology, the study of weather. Computers were just beginning to appear in science labs. Lorenz wanted to use his brand new LGP-30 computer to figure out methods for predicting the weather.

The computer came with a 64-page manual. Both he and Margaret poured over it, cover to cover, to understand how to use the huge machine.

"Lorenz gave me all the freedom I needed in order to experiment with new ways to do things," recalls Margaret. "He loved working with his computer." Together, Lorenz and Margaret were able to decipher the complexities of computers.

She was absolutely fascinated. The professor encouraged his young co-worker to create new programs.

Margaret stated, in a 2018 speech that Lorenz was "known as a genius by his colleagues, his love for software experimentation was contagious." She added, "We worked a lot on finding better techniques to make the computer go faster. . . . Errors were a nuisance. Each debug session took forever."

As the 1960s began, Margaret was learning more and more about how to use a computer. That was no easy task. At that time, there were no classes or books on how to use them, just a user's manual. There were no experts to ask. Computers were just too new and too unfamiliar. Everything Margaret

Margaret was a part of Project Whirlwind, a system intended for pilot training. This led to MIT's first computer which occupied 2,500 square feet of space in MIT's Barta Building.

learned about computers was self-taught through experimenting and trial and error.

"When I first got into it," Margaret stated in an interview with *Wired* magazine, "nobody knew what it was that we were doing. It was like the Wild West."

Margaret spent months working on Project Whirlwind. The team planned to use the Whirlwind system for pilot training. It would be more advanced than any training system used before.

In order to qualify for the team, Margaret had to pass the test given to all new team members. The test was kept secret, but everyone knew it was considered an almost unsolvable program. It was complicated.

"What they used to do . . . was to assign you this program which nobody was ever able to figure out or get to run," stated Margaret at a Caltech University conference. "When I was a beginner, they gave it to me as well. And what had happened," she continued, "was it was tricky programming, and the person who wrote it took delight in the fact that all of his comments were in Greek and Latin. . . . It even printed out its answers in Latin and Greek."

So far, no students had been able to get the program to work—until Margaret, that is.

"I was the first one to get it to work," she stated. "You can see the overriding theme here; I was and still am very interested in what causes errors and how to avoid them throughout. That was one of my very first experiences in this regard."

CHAPTER FOUR

SAGE

The enormous halls of SAGE computers were used as dramatic props in Hollywood movies, especially those set during the Cold War.

The IBM AN/FSQ-7 computers used for SAGE (Semi-Automatic Ground Environment) were huge. They weighed 275 tons. They used 55,000 vacuum tubes. A single computer needed a half acre of room, often taking up an entire warehouse. The computers were kept deep inside the lower levels of MIT's Lincoln Lab.

It was not long before the focus of Margaret's work began to change. As part of SAGE at MIT, she created programs for the computer that would allow it to identify enemy aircraft.

A vaccum tube is a device that controls the flow of engery in an enclosed, airless space.

By recognizing Soviet Union bombers, the US could prepare to defend itself against possible attacks. At the time, America was involved in the Cold War. The Soviet Union was the country's top foe. In these early days of computers, code was first recorded on coding sheets. These patterns were transferred to thousands and thousands of punch cards.

When the IBM computer ran into an error in the code, a sound like sirens and foghorns would

Women in the 1960s were frequently typists, which meant women were in charge of entering code and became very good at spotting errors.

blast through the building. Lights would flash. Everyone came running to fix the problem. Margaret hated these moments. Sometimes she was called back to work in the middle of the night to fix something.

"It became a way of being and doing," she described to *The Earlhamite*, Earlham College's magazine. "I was determined not to let something like that happen again," she stated. It became Margaret's mission, then and for the rest of her life, to help prevent computer errors.

From 1961 to 1963, Margaret worked on the SAGE project. During this time, she began using the little known term "software engineer" to describe her job. Software was Margaret's specialty. When she first used the term, her co-workers would chuckle. Few suspected that one day software would be one of the most important and fastest-growing fields in technology.

"Software during the early days of this project was...not taken as seriously as other engineering disciplines, such as hardware engineering; and it was regarded as an art and as magic, not a science," she stated. "I had always believed that both art and science were involved in its creation, but at that time most thought otherwise."

In an interview with *Medium* magazine, she stated, "When I first started using this phrase [software engineer], it was considered to be quite amusing. It was an ongoing joke for a long time. They liked to kid me about my radical ideas," she added. "Software eventually and necessarily gained the same respect as any other discipline."

During these years at SAGE, Margaret would often bring Lauren to work with her in the lab in the evenings or on weekends. The toddler grew up surrounded by the lights and sounds of computers.

Lauren frequently slept on the floor of her mother's office. Bringing a child to work is not considered terribly odd today, but in the early 1960s, it was almost unheard of.

In 1958, President Dwight Eisenhower signed the public order titled Space Act. This created NASA, providing the government with an official agency focusing on ways to explore space.

Among NASA's goals was to work in "close cooperation among all interested agencies of the United States" so that their mission to space could be fruitful. One of those agencies was MIT.

MIT worked with NASA in 1961 to develop the Apollo program's guidance system. Margaret was a part of MIT's team and worked long hours. She, along with the rest of her team at MIT and NASA, was determined to send man to the Moon.

CHAPTER FIVE

Into the Space Race

Part of the reason Gagarin was chosen was his small stature. He was five feet, two inches tall, which meant he could fit in the small cockpit easily.

For the next two years, the race truly was on. First, the Russians sent up a second space probe. Then, in 1961, it was followed by the first manned-rocket flight.

Cosmonaut Yuri Gagarin orbited the Earth in a rocket called the *Vostok 1* for 108 minutes. However, America was close behind.

In September 1962, new President John F. Kennedy, gave his "Moon Speech" at Rice University in Texas. It inspired people of all ages to look up to the sky and imagine what might be up there.

In his speech, he stated, "We choose to go to the Moon. We choose to go to the Moon in this decade and do the other things, not because they are easy, but because they are hard, because that goal will serve to organize and measure the best of our energies and skills, because that challenge is one that we are willing to accept, one we are unwilling to postpone, and one which we intend to win."

President Kennedy made it clear that the effort to get into space was going to be one of the biggest priorities of his presidency. He planned to get a man on the Moon by the end of the 1960s. Tragically, he did not live long enough to see his dream come true.

At the end of his speech, he added, "Many years

ago the great British explorer George Mallory, who was to die on Mount Everest, was asked why did he want to climb it. He said, 'Because it is there.' Well, space is there, and we're going to climb it, and the Moon and the planets are there, and new hopes for knowledge and peace are there."

John F. Kennedy was the youngest President of the United States at 43 years old.

In 1961, Alan B. Shepard Jr. went into space, becoming the first American in space. Less than a year later, John H. Glenn Jr. became the first American to orbit Earth. For the next several years, more money was given to NASA to develop better spaceships, train astronauts, and create bigger projects.

NASA employed more than 34,000 people. One of these employees turned out to be an amazing mathematician and software engineer: Margaret Hamilton. Up until then, she had worked primarily on weather predictions and weapons tracking.

The ICSE provides a place for researchers and educators to present and discuss software. It's a place for software engineering to grow.

In August 1961, MIT's Charles Stark Draper Laboratory (CSDL) was given a contract from NASA to develop computer guidance and control systems. The Apollo spaceships would need these systems to fly to the Moon and back.

There was little question that Margaret wanted to be part of the team that would work on this amazing project. She decided to delay going back to graduate school, because she wanted the chance to work on sending men to the Moon.

"The challenge was unique," she told the audience at the 40th Annual International Conference on Software Engineering (ICSE) held in Sweden in June 2018. She was the ICSE's keynote speaker at the age of 82. "It [the software] had to work and it had to work the first time."

She knew that it would be an incredible opportunity.

"My experience working for NASA and MIT was a one-of-a-kind, once-in-a-lifetime experience," Margaret said years later. "Whatever I might say to describe this experience would not do it justice."

Lucky for Margaret—and for the Apollo missions

and NASA—she got the job! She would be the only woman on her team, but that did not bother her. Together, they would work on computer coding for the inside of spacecrafts.

"Women were always in the minority and men were always in the majority," she told *Futurism* magazine. "But more than anything," she continued, "we were dedicated to the missions and worked side-by-side to solve the challenging problems and to meet the critical deadlines."

Margaret said that she was so focused on her work that she did not think about being one of the only women. "We concentrated on our work much more than whether one was male or female," she added.

There was one moment when Margaret was briefly aware that men and women had different challenges. When one female MIT worker wanted to get a credit union loan, she was rejected. She was told she could not get one without her husband's approval. Margaret complained. "So I went to the credit union at MIT and I told them, 'This is not fair.' And the credit union was made up of mostly men but some women and the men all agreed with me that the rules should be changed." The policy was changed.

"It was the culture but I won, and I was so happy," she stated. "I didn't do it because of male versus female," she added. "I was very conscious of what was fair and what wasn't fair."

Around the same time, a movement for gender equality was gaining speed. The second-wave feminist movement believed that women should be equal to men.

First-wave feminism worked to get women legal rights. The right to vote and the right to own property were the biggest concerns of the earlier movement.

Second-wave feminism was more interested in equal pay, equality in the workplace, and the fight against domestic violence. Margaret was helping by changing policies that treated women differently than men. She also made sure to include female scientists and programmers when she could, opening the door for other women.

Other NASA women did similar things to help fellow scientists. Jeanette Scissum was a mathematician and worked to analyse space environment data. She also volunteered to work as NASA's Equal Employment Opportunity officer.

Mary Jackson was highlighted in the feature film *Hidden Figures*. She worked her way up to the highest level in the engineering department before opting to be demoted to become an Equal Opportunity Specialist. From there, she was able to support and highlight the achievements of women and minority groups.

The steps these women took to ensure gender equality impacted the current culture of society

Many women worked alongside Margaret and the early NASA teams including (l to r) Mary Jackson, Dorothy Vaughan, and Katherine Johnson.

today. It is because of these women that we have seen improvements in the treatment of all in the workplace.

CHAPTER SIX

Leader of the Pack

By 1965, Margaret had moved from team member to team director. That meant she was in charge of more than one hundred engineers, mathematicians, programmers, and technical writers. At the age of 29, that was remarkable.

It was Margaret's team that was responsible for writing the code needed for the Apollo spacecraft to land on the Moon safely. The software would be used in the lunar module, the part of the spacecraft that touched down on the Moon. It would also be used on the command module, the spacecraft section that orbited the Moon and then carried the crew of astronauts home.

Each one of these portable computers weighed about 70 pounds. They were some of the first computerized onboard navigation systems. Project

Gemini had the first onboard computers, but they were only used sometimes. Project Apollo was the first to use computers during all phases of the mission.

In 1965, Margaret officially became responsible for the onboard flight software on the Apollo computers that operated the lunar and command modules.

Don Eyles, one of Margaret's co-workers at MIT, stated, "It was the first time that an important computer had been in a spacecraft and given a lot of responsibility for the mission. We showed that it could be done."

Amazingly, most of this code was first written

with pencil and paper. From there, it was put on coding sheets. Then, it was sent to the keypunchers. The team wrote books and books of code.

For every decision made, as well as every single line of code, Margaret and others had to write full explanations of why, what it did, and how it affected the entire program. Piled up, the code books were almost as tall as Margaret.

Code was transferred to punch cards by a team of women. These women were trained to read and translate the code and were in charge of taking care of the punch cards. The cards couldn't get wet at

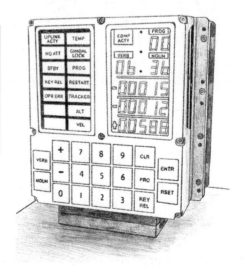

The computers that took people to the Moon worked on 64 kilobytes of memory. Today's cellphones have 31,000 times more memory than those computers did.

Margaret said about the code, "from my perspective, the software experience itself was at least as exciting as the events surrounding the mission."

all or they would be useless. Also, a single mistyped card could ruin an entire program. Accuracy was key.

Each card held one instruction for the computer. The more complicated the program, the more cards were needed.

These cards, in turn, were fed into the computer by computer operators. The coding was then printed out and put into thick binders.

What happened if there was a problem with the code? The team would have to stop everything and write it all over again—by hand.

Minor problems with code were often called "FLTs" or "Funny Little Things" by Margaret's team. To repair these mistakes required the "Auge Kugel" method.

"When Margaret first heard people referring to the "Auge Kugel" method, she was confused. "I can't tell them that I don't know what this method is that everyone is using," she thought. Finally she got the courage to ask. "It was simply 'eyeballing'

Margaret was interested in debugging systems, and found sound to be a helpful tool. Her SAGE program was made to sound like a seashore. When the sound stopped, Margaret knew she had to get to work.

The programming for SAGE was stored on thousands of small punch cards. The programming for the Apollo missions took even more.

in German," she said with a chuckle.

In other words, the way anything was repaired was to look closely at it and try to read it as if you were a computer.

As she had been doing for years, Margaret focused on making sure that her code did not include any errors. One night, when she suddenly suspected she had written something wrong, she rushed back to the lab to correct it.

"I was always imagining headlines in the newspapers," she stated, "and they would point back to how it happened, and it would point back to me."

Writing code to be used in the Apollo missions meant that all of her data was "man-rated." As she said in the ICSE speech in 2018, "Man-rated means if something doesn't work, a man's life is at stake—or even over."

An error in this type of coding meant far more than just blaring alarms and blinking lights. It meant that astronauts could be in danger or even lose their lives.

Margaret and her team relied strongly on trial and error when creating their software. As Margaret wrote in one of her papers:

When there were no answers to be found, at times we just had to make it up, and we had to design things to work the first time.

. . Learning was by doing . . . and a dramatic event would often dictate change. Because software was a mystery, a black box, upper management gave us total freedom and trust. . . Looking back, we were the luckiest people in the world. There was no choice but to be pioneers; no time to be beginners.

CHAPTER SEVEN

"Forget It"

Over her years at MIT, Margaret continued to bring Lauren to work with her. This was decades before any workplace had bring your child to work programs. Many people thought it was quite

Margaret and James divorced in 1967, making it difficult for Margaret to spend both time with her daughter and remain dedicated to the Apollo project.

odd, but Margaret did not care. She was trying to balance being a mother with having an amazingly demanding job.

"I made sure to spend as much time as possible with my daughter by taking her to work with me during nights and weekends," explained Margaret to the PTC website. It was a good thing she did too, because, thanks to Lauren playing games in Margaret's office, the crew of *Apollo 8* made it back to earth alive.

In order to create computers to be used on the Apollo missions, the MIT team had to create simulations, in the lab. This would allow Margaret and others to run code and make sure the computers performed each operation correctly.

"We had to simulate everything before it flew," Hamilton told *Wired* magazine.

One day, six-year-old Lauren was playing inside one of the Apollo simulators known as the DSKY or "dis-key."

"She [Lauren] got very interested in wanting to play astronaut," recalled Margaret.

She pushed a new button. It launched a

prelaunch program known as P01. Having a prelaunch program start when the simulator was supposed to be midflight was a disaster. An error message popped up immediately. The computer crashed.

If that had happened during an actual Apollo mission, the rocket would likely have also crashed. Naturally, Margaret wanted to add code to the

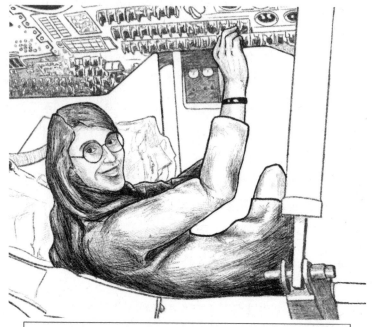

Computer programming took creativity and out-of-the-box thinking. Programmers have to find ways to fix issues with tight deadlines.

computer program that would prevent this disaster from actually happening.

For years, her passion had been writing code that would rule out any errors. However, her NASA and MIT colleagues did not always agree.

"I think we need to make a change in there asking if this was a good time P01 should be used," she told NASA.

No, not needed, NASA responded. Their astronauts were experts. They were too highly trained to worry about making such an error as this one. Margaret still had her doubts.

"Many of the things I was intrigued by had to do with how to make the mission software safe and reliable," she said at the 2001 Conference of the Apollo Guidance Computer History Project.

"And one of the things I remember trying very hard to do was to get permission to be able to put more error detection and recovery into the software. So that if the astronaut made a mistake, the software would come back and say 'You can't do that.' But we were forbidden to put that software in because it was more software to debug, to work with.

"So one of the things that we were really worried about is what if the astronaut made a mistake. We were also told that the astronauts would never make any mistakes, because they were trained never to make mistakes."

Pilot Jim Lovell has gone into space four separate times and logged over 700 hours there.

"So we were very worried that what if the astronaut, during mid-course, would select pre-launch, for example? 'Never would happen,' they said. 'Never would happen.'

It happened.

In President Kennedy's famous space race speech, he stated that he wanted to see humans landing on the Moon by the end of the 1960s. In December of 1968, *Apollo 8* carried the first humans to orbit the Moon but did not land. The flight set a new world speed record of 24,200 miles per hour.

The spacecraft orbited the Moon ten times on Christmas Eve. On Christmas morning, Mission Control gave the official command to return home. Astronaut Lovell replied, "Roger, please be informed there is a Santa Claus."

Unfortunately, on the fifth day of the mission, Command Module Pilot Jim Lovell did the exact thing that Margaret had worried about. He hit P01 by accident. The mission was in big trouble.

Since she was not allowed to fix the computer's programming to prevent the P01 button from crashing the computer, Margaret did the next best thing. She added a note to the software that basically said "Do not select P01 during flight."

She intentionally called her project "Forget It," because no one believed it would ever be needed or used.

Now, after the touch of one wrong button, the route home was in danger of being lost.

Hamilton was in the lab when the emergency call from Mission Control came through. The *Apollo 8* crew reported that the program had just wiped out all of the navigation data Lovell had been using. Without that information, the Apollo computer would not be able to bring Lovell, Lunar Module Pilot William Anders, and Commander Frank Borman back home.

Everyone scrambled. Hamilton and her team spent an intense nine hours going through

The *Apollo 8 astronauts safely landed in the ocean, but the accidental loss of the navigation data backed up Margaret's argument for just-in-case programming.*

a huge binder of data. Finally, they came up with a plan to upload new navigational data to the Apollo's computers.

It worked. The mission was a success! On December 27, 1968, the crew of *Apollo 8* splashed down in the Pacific Ocean safely. Later, NASA made the wise decision that Margaret's note should be included in all future flights—just in case.

It took Margaret's team nine hours to come up with a plan after the navigational data was wiped.

Margaret's passion for finding and fixing errors before they could cause problems—and Lauren playing around in the lab—hadn't saved the day, but they would be allowed to prevent future life-threatening mistakes.

CHAPTER EIGHT

A Moment in Time

An estimated one million people watched the Apollo 11 *lauch in person, while twenty-five million more watched it live on television.*

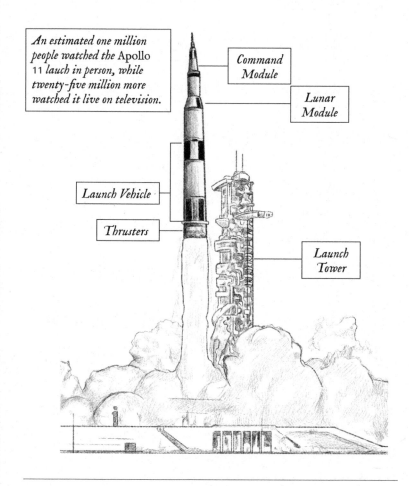

Command Module

Lunar Module

Launch Vehicle

Thrusters

Launch Tower

The *Apollo 11* mission started it's 238,855 mile journey to the Moon at 1:32 pm on July 16, 1969. A crater named "The Sea of Tranquility" was chosen as the landing spot on the Moon. Given its mostly flat surface, it was the ideal place to attempt to land the lunar module.

Three minutes before the lunar module Eagle was supposed to touch down at the Sea of Tranquility, alarms began ringing. Yellow lights flashed.

Michael Collins, who was steering the command module, recalled hearing the alarm code 1202 from Neil Armstrong. While he did not have the alarm codes memorized, Mission Control in Houston, Texas was quick to step in.

Houston says, "Roger, we're GO on that alarm." No problem, in other words.

A 1202 alarm code is an "executive overflow." This means the computer has been asked to perform too many tasks at once, causing it to postpone some of them.

Then another alarm buzzes. This time, it's a 1201,

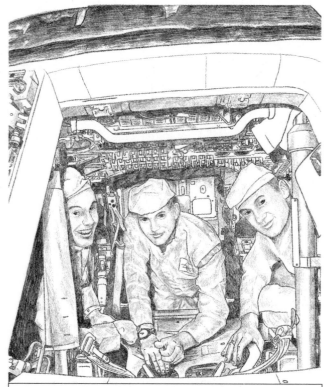

The command module was small, so no space was wasted. It was very close quarters, but Armstrong, Collins, and Aldrin could fit.

another overflow alarm. Mission Control reassures the space crew to keep moving forward, but they were all waiting to see what would happen. This was the most crucial part of the mission, landing on the surface of the Moon, yet the computer was having trouble tackling too many calculations at once.

Margaret knew exactly what was happening. She was standing in Draper Labs when the alarms went off.

"Once it was time for liftoff, I focused on the software and how it was performing throughout each and every part of the mission. Everything was going according to plan until something totally unexpected happened, just as the astronauts were in the process of landing on the Moon," she recalled in an interview with *MIT News*.

"I was standing in the [lab] listening to the conversations between the astronauts and Mission Control when all of a sudden the normal mission sequences were interrupted by priority displays of 1201 and 1202 alarms, giving the astronauts a go/ no go decision (to land or not to land)," stated Margaret.

"I looked across the room at Fred Martin and

he [looked] back at me. What could possibly cause these alarms to be triggered at this most crucial time? It quickly became clear that the software

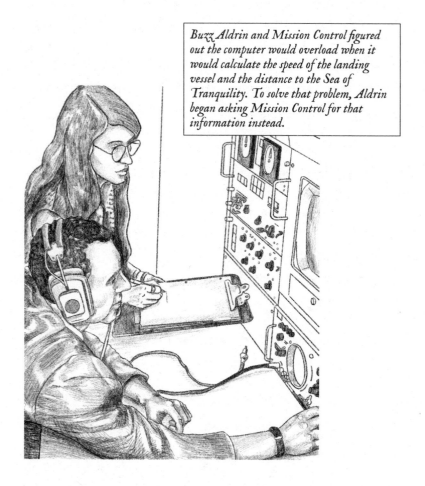

Buzz Aldrin and Mission Control figured out the computer would overload when it would calculate the speed of the landing vessel and the distance to the Sea of Tranquility. To solve that problem, Aldrin began asking Mission Control for that information instead.

was not only informing everyone that there was a hardware-related problem, but that the software was compensating for it."

Fortunately, Margaret and her team had programmed the computer to put its many tasks in the order of importance. Although the alarms were still going, NASA had to decide whether to tell the Apollo crew to abort, or stop, the mission, or to ignore the yellow lights and keep landing.

As Margaret said, "With only minutes to spare, the decision was made to go for the landing. The rest is history... There was no second chance. We knew that."

When *Apollo 11* finally landed on the crater known as Sea of Tranquility, they told mission control "Houston, Tranquility Base here. The Eagle has landed."

Houston's response showed just how worried everyone had been. They said, "Roger, Tranquility. We copy you on the ground. You've got a bunch of guys about to turn blue. We're breathing again. Thanks a lot."

Minutes later, they added, "Be advised there's [a] lot of smiling faces in this room and all over the world."

Located in Building 30 of the Johnson Space Center, this facility was used as Mission Control for the nine Gemini missions and all of the Apollo missions.

President Kennedy's goal was achieved on July 20, 1969. As astronaut Neil Armstrong stepped out of the spaceship and onto the Moon, he uttered the famous words, "That's one small step for man, one giant leap for mankind."

Millions of people all over the world watched as black and white images of the Moon filled their television screens. Sadly, JFK, the president who set the goal for the United States to reach the Moon by 1970, was not able to share this moment of triumph. He had been assassinated on November 22, 1963.

The Moon Landing was the most watched event on television for over a decade. However, its viewership record was beat in 1981 with the televised wedding of Prince Charles and Lady Diana.

The *Apollo 11* mission was a huge success. Astronauts Neil Armstrong and Buzz Aldrin spent a total of 21 hours and 36 minutes on the Moon's surface. They planted an American flag and collected rock samples.

Four days after leaving Earth, the crew splashed down in the Pacific Ocean. The astronauts were heroes! The United States had achieved something no other nation had been able to do. They put humans on the Moon.

CHAPTER NINE

Potential Catastrophe

Newspaper headlines shouted out the success of the *Apollo 11* mission. The astronauts were interviewed on television and appeared in magazines. Various people at NASA were asked what was next for space exploration.

The mission to the Moon had an impact on pop culture as well. David Bowie's song "Space Oddity" was played by the BBC when it covered the Moon landing.

Other famous bands of the time created space-related songs. Creedence Clearwater Revival

Margaret's fears were calmed as newspapers reported on the successful mission to the Moon.

had "Bad Moon Rising," Jonathan King sang "Everyone's Gone to the Moon," and Pink Floyd created an album titled *The Dark Side of the Moon*.

Filmmaker Stanley Kubrick created *2001: A Space Odyssey* in 1968, a movie where a hostile computer terrorizes an astronaut. It highlighted a fear of the rising technology that came with the mission to the Moon.

Around the same time, the Hanna-Barbera cartoon *The Jetsons* ran on prime time TV. It featured a family living in the future driving flying cars and employing a robot maid. After the Moon landing, many people thought that the cartoon would become reality.

Fashion designers began displaying the Moon girl look. Mini skirts, go-go boots, and oversized sunglasses were key elements of the style. Many outfits also featured large geometric shapes and helmets or headwear.

Everyone was looking to the future, including Margaret. She was more than ready to keep improving Apollo computers and making sure that space missions were successful—and safe.

Long after the *Apollo 11* crew was safely back on earth, it was found that the alarms had been due to what was called a "checklist error."

One of the crew had pushed a switch to start a system that was needed to leave the Moon. The

Staff members posed with the landing capsule as a souvenir and keepsake for their families.

system was confused and sent out alarms. It was Hamilton's software that helped the computer focus on setting the lunar module down on the Moon as directed.

Plans were already in place for future missions to the Moon, as well as a large deep-space telescope. People were even starting to think about the possibility of humans living on the Moon or other planets.

"*Apollo 11* was the most memorable of all of my memorable experiences," Margaret has stated. "It was both a relief and a wonderful feeling as soon as the landing on the Moon took place."

CHAPTER TEN

NASA and Beyond

After *Apollo 11*, it was clear that Margaret's software not only worked, but could save lives. For several years, she stayed with NASA working on other Apollo missions.

Between 1969 and 1972, six manned flights went into space. *Apollo 12* launched on November 14, 1969. Its 10-day mission was followed by *Apollo 13* on April 11, 1970.

Unlike *Apollo 11* and *12*, the *Apollo 13* mission ran into trouble on the way to the Moon. When equipment failure made it impossible to stay in the command module, the crew had to move into the lunar module.

It was crowded. Oxygen was limited. The entire

world watched what was happening on television. People worried that the crew would not make it back to earth.

Fortunately, the three men splashed back down early on April 17. They were disappointed they did not get the chance to walk on the Moon, but were grateful just to get back home.

Apollo 14 went to the Moon on January 31, 1971. The crew landed safely at a spot called Fra Mauro.

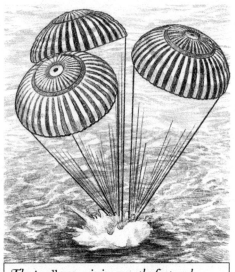

The Apollo 13 *mission was the first and only Apollo mission to be aborted mid-flight, ending with a splashdown in the Pacific Ocean.*

It was the same site *Apollo 13* had planned to use. While there, Commander Alan Shepard Jr., stopped to hit a couple golf balls off the Moon's surface.

Later the same year, in July, *Apollo 15* lifted off from Kennedy Space Center. This eight-day mission was the first one to use the LRV, or lunar roving vehicle. It helped astronauts explore more surface area on the Moon. It also carried tools, scientific equipment, communication gear, and soil and rock samples.

NASA wanted a trained geologist to land on the Moon to collect samples. They chose Harrison Schmitt.

On April 16, 1972, *Apollo 16* headed for the Moon. The mission lasted 11 days. It was followed by *Apollo 17* on December 7, 1972. After landing on the Moon, launch module pilot Harrison Schmitt collected rock and soil samples. Schmitt was the first geologist to be on the Moon.

The team explored more of the Moon, thanks to the use of the LRV. *Apollo 17*'s mission was the longest one. It lasted more than 12 days and was the final Apollo mission.

Much of the software Margaret had developed for *Apollo 11* was used in the following space missions. Some of it was also used in space shuttle flights and in Skylab, the world's first space station.

Skylab was launched into orbit on May 14, 1973. It was four stories tall, weighed more than 100 tons, and was 22-feet in diameter.

Skylab was built so that crews of astronauts could live and work in space for weeks at a time. It had sections designed for sleeping, eating, and working. It even had an area with exercise equipment so the

Skylab was in orbit for six years, housing three different three-man crews who conducted more than 270 experiments.

astronauts could stay fit.

Three different crews stayed in the Skylab space station. All together, these three crews spent 171 days and 13 hours at Skylab. In addition to doing hundreds of different experiments in the space station, experts also studied how weeks spent in space affected the human body.

One of Skylab's main missions was to learn more about the sun. More than 120,000 photographs were taken by the ship's camera.

After Skylab was no longer being used by crews, it was left to orbit the earth until it fell apart. That happened in 1979. The debris came back down to earth on July 11, 1979. Parts fell over the Indian Ocean and in parts of Western Australia.

In 1976, Margaret made a big decision. She thought it was time for her to move on from her work at NASA. That year, she founded her own company, along with co-worker Dan Lickly. It was called Higher Order Software.

The debris of Skylab (shown here) landed in places like farm fields, roads in Western Australia, and the Indian Ocean.

CHAPTER ELEVEN

Branching Out

As with her earlier work at MIT and NASA, Margaret's work at Higher Order Software focused on creating software that allowed no room for error. One of the programs she developed was named simply USE.IT. It was used in a number of military and government computer systems.

Margaret worked with Higher Order Software until 1985. Then she felt the need for another change. She created Hamilton Technologies in Cambridge, Massachusetts the following year.

As the CEO of the company, Margaret focused on creating what she called a "universal systems language." Not surprisingly, this program was focused on preventing errors before they occurred.

The companies of today seem to go by Zuckerberg's motto "move fast and break things." Higher Order Software, however, worked toward creating reliable software the first time to lessen the probability of problems later.

As she put it, "As time went on, I got very interested, even more and more interested in error detection and recovery, because of the errors that took place and how we could avoid them in the first place."

Through Hamilton Technologies, Margaret shared her ideas with others, including companies such as Boeing, IBM, Hewlett Packard, and even the US Navy.

The same year that Margaret started Hamilton Technologies, she was given the Ada Lovelace Award by the Association for Women in Computing. The award is named after Augusta Ada Byron Lovelace, history's first official computer programmer.

Ada Lovelace lived from 1815–1852 in England where she was a writer and mathematician. She has been honored by the STEM community which deemed the second Tuesday of October "Ada Lovelace Day."

Lovelace was the only daughter of poet Lord Byron and his wife. She was a mathematician in the early nineteenth century and the first person to realize that computers could be more than calculators.

Lovelace was also the first to create an algorithm for a computer. An algorithm is a list of yes or no questions that tells a computer what to do. For example, an algorithm for chores might look like this:

1. Did you take the trash out?

    If yes, put your laundry in the hamper and proceed to question 2.

    If no, go take the trash out and return to question 1.

2. Did you put your laundry in the hamper?

    If yes, you can go play video games!

    If no, go put your laundry in the hamper and return to question 2.

Ada Lovelace is largely recognized as the first

person to realize how powerful computers could be. She worked with Charles Babbage, the "father of computers," on the Analytical Engine, the first computer.

The Ada Lovelace Award is given to people who have excelled in one or both of two areas. First is for outstanding scientific and technical achievement. Second is for extraordinary service to the computing community through accomplishments and contributions on behalf of women in computing.

By now, Margaret was no longer married to James Hamilton. He had gone on to become a well-known lawyer in Boston.

After starting his own law firm in 1969, he spent his life defending people's rights. He was the lawyer on many cases for the American Civil Liberties Union. His co-workers described him as gentle and kind. One stated that Hamilton was "willing to speak out for the underdog, but he did it through the force of his logic, rather than the volume of his voice."

Her daughter Lauren was grown. She had gotten married in 1982 to actor and dancer James Cox Chambers. She later divorced and remarried to Richard Selesnick. Lauren made a career for herself as an actress and makeup artist in Hollywood.

Divorced from James, her daughter grown, and NASA in her past—what was next for Margaret?

Margaret's ex-husband, James Cox Hamilton, worked as a lawyer until his death and was honored as a beloved mentor.

CHAPTER TWELVE

In Honor of Her Work

When Margaret walked onto the stage at the 2018 ICSE conference, it was hard to believe she was 82. As the keynote speaker, she stood and spoke to the audience for more than an hour about her time as a software engineer with MIT, SAGE, and NASA.

She chuckled, recalling how much more primitive the field was back then. "A manager hired you if you 'knew' the commands in his computer's native language," she stated. "Like 'knowing' a set of English words would mean you could write a novel."

A number of female audience members thanked Margaret for being a role model for them. Her impact on the world of science was a lesson to the world that women were intelligent, skilled, and determined.

"To make real change, much more needs to

Margaret recieved two honorary doctorates from Polytechnic University and Bard College for her groundbreaking work in software engineering.

be done," Margaret said of the ongoing battle for women to have science careers.

"When the most powerful and influential leaders and organizations in the world make it possible for women to hold the highest positions (not "almost" the highest) in their organizations, equal (not "almost" equal) to what is available to men, we all benefit; including the leaders and organizations themselves."

Since opening Hamilton Technologies in 1986, Margaret has kept busy. She continues to write papers and give speeches. She has received a number of honors also.

In 2003, NASA gave her the Exceptional Space Act Award for the work she and her team provided during the Apollo missions.

"The Apollo flight software Ms. Hamilton and her team developed was truly a pioneering effort," stated NASA administrator Sean O'Keefe. "The concepts she and her team created became the building blocks for modern 'software engineering.' It's an honor to recognize Ms. Hamilton for her extraordinary contributions to NASA."

It was Dr. Paul Curto who nominated Margaret for the NASA Exceptional Space Act award. He

When Margaret recieved the Exceptional Space Act Award from NASA, administrator Sean O'Keefe stated, "The Apollo flight software Ms. Hamilton and her team developed was truly a pioneering effort"

stated that he "was surprised to realize she was never formally recognized for her groundbreaking work."

He added that many of the computer programming concepts she discovered ended up as the foundation for today's software design. This cash award of $37,200 was the largest one that NASA had given to an individual person.

In 2009, Margaret was honored by her former

college, Earlham. She was given the Outstanding Alumni award.

Then, in 2016, Margaret was given one of the biggest awards in the United States. On November 22, she was awarded the Presidential Medal of Freedom by President Barack Obama.

The Presidential Medal of Freedom is only awarded to people who have contributed a great deal to the security or national interests of the US,

Margaret was honored for "[setting] the foundation for modern, ultra-reliable software design and engineering."

Margaret, who worked on code for the Apollo missions, was honored at the same time as Tom Hanks, who played astronaut Jim Lovell in the movie Apollo 13.

as well as to those who work for world peace.

It was established by JFK in 1963, replacing the original Medal of Freedom created in 1945 by President Truman. While the original Medal of Freedom honored civilian service during World War II, the current medal honors civilians in numerous fields. People in the arts, sciences, sports, business, and politics fields have earned this honor.

In 1969, astronauts Neil Armstrong, Michael Collins, and Buzz Aldrin were given these medals by President Richard Nixon. In 2016, actor Tom Hanks, who played astronaut Jim Lovell in the 1995 film, *Apollo 13* was also given the medal. When Margaret was announced at the ceremony, President Obama stated, that she "symbolizes that

Margaret has been honored many times for her work with NASA. In 2019, the search engine Google created an art installation in her honor. The company set up more than 100,000 mirrors in a remote desert in a particular sequence. Once the Moon rose, its light reflected on the mirrors, creating a portrait of Margaret and the Apollo 11 spacecraft.

generation of unsung women who helped send humankind into space."

He added that, "her example speaks of the American spirit of discovery that exists in every little girl and little boy who knows that somehow to look beyond the heavens is to look deep within ourselves and to figure out just what is possible."

The following year, Margaret received the 2017 Computer History Museum Fellow Award. The goal of this award is to honor people whose computing skills and ideas have changed the world.

CHAPTER THIRTEEN

A Strong Role Model

In November 2017, Margaret was honored in two completely different ways. First, in 2016, Maia Weinstock, the deputy editor of *MIT News*, from the university, proposed a new idea to the LEGO toy company. She thought they should create a set of NASA's most famous female scientists and astronauts.

"So I thought [the project] would be a perfect combination of highlighting women in STEM and also highlighting women who have contributed greatly to NASA," explained Weinstock to Space. com.

She suggested that the set feature four women. The first was Nancy Grace Roman, also known as the "Mother of Hubble." She was one of the most important members on the team that created the Hubble Space Telescope.

After retiring, Margaret turned her focus to spending time with her family and encouraging other young women to follow their dreams and do amazing things.

Second and third, Weinstock suggested Sally Ride, the first American woman in space, and Mae Jemison, the first African-American woman in space. Her fourth suggestion was for Margaret Hamilton.

"I decided to work on specific women, instead of generic women," stated Weinstock. "Because I thought this would be something different. And this is something I am passionate about, which is bringing [STEM] personalities to light. It was a risk. I mean, nothing like this has ever been posted [to LEGO Ideas] before, at least in terms of women."

Within 15 days of the idea being posted online, it had gotten more than 10,000 supporters. "The set clearly touched and inspired many," said Weinstock. On her blog, Weinstock described the reasons for why she chose Roman, Ride, Jemison, and Hamilton. She stated that she wanted to choose women that were involved in all aspects of NASA's missions.

"Another consideration was that I didn't want this set to focus solely on space travelers," she wrote on her blog.

"I designed it also to honor and recognize some of the women who've been underappreciated for their critical work behind the scenes, as computer scientists, as mathematicians, as engineers, and more."

She added, "At the end of the day, while this project features four individuals, the spirit of the Women of NASA LEGO set is meant to honor all women who've contributed in some way to the agency's mission of advancing society through space exploration."

When the set was released by LEGO, it was a huge seller. Margaret's figure has glasses and long hair. It comes with a stack of books from the world famous photo of her standing next to the stack of coding binders. Her face piece has two sides: one serious and one smiling. In her hand is a newspaper

Within 24 hours of its release, the LEGO "Women of NASA" sets became bestsellers. Margaret's set reflects her famous photograph standing next to the Apollo code binders.

announcing "Men Walk on Moon."

What does Margaret think of having a LEGO that looks like her? She says that she is pleased, because "at least my great-grandchildren will know a little bit about me."

Margaret has been awarded honorary doctorates

from two different Universities. The Polytechnic University of Catalonia in Spain honored her in 2018. The next year, Bard College in New York, where her daughter had attended, also gave her an honorary doctorate degree.

In 2019, she was given the Intrepid Lifetime Achievement Award. This award was established to recognize people for lifetime and pioneering achievements.

Margaret thought the LEGOs were a great way to get young girls interested in science.

Earlham president David Dawson issued a statement letting Margaret know how proud the college was of her achievements:

> On behalf of the entire Earlham community, I congratulate Margaret Hamilton on this incredible and well deserved honor. Margaret is a wonderful example of what we hope for all Earlhamites: that they will be able to . . . contribute to positive change in the world.
>
> In particular, she is an inspiration to young women scientists who can look at her as a reminder for what is possible. Her incredible accomplishments make us all proud to be Earlhamites.

In 2022, Margaret was inducted into the National Aviation Hall of Fame, an organization that honors the country's aerospace pioneers.

Other NASA enshrinees include James Lovell, Gus Grissom, and Buzz Aldrin.

In addition, all of Margaret's software collection, including her extensive software programs, field notes, and flight plans, have been added to the Smithsonian's National Air and Space Museum. Visitors to the museum have been able to see the Margaret Hamilton display as soon as they walk in. The Computer History Museum also included Margaret as an avatar in their new Minecraft: Education Edition.

Certainly she will keep inspiring young people, as President Obama stated, "to look deep within ourselves and to figure out just what is possible." Like her father and grandfather before her, she inspires everyone to ask "what if" and keep asking until the answers are found.

As Margaret herself advised, "Don't be afraid to question things and don't be afraid to ask so-called stupid questions. . . I'd always say never say never . . and never give up." She added that just because someone is told their idea is not going to work, do not give up. "If you can't solve it, put it in a different place . . and don't be afraid to disagree with the experts," she added.

Margaret Hamilton still lives in Indiana today, although she gives speeches throughout the world.

"One should not be afraid to say 'I don't know' or 'I don't understand,' or to ask 'dumb' questions, since no question is a dumb question."

Margaret Hamilton

"The type of experience and education one has before entering the fields of STEM as well as other fields is key. . . . Learning how to work with and getting used to being around different kinds of personalities and challenges helps one to have the flexibility needed to understand others, and to deal with the unexpected."

Margaret Hamilton

"Regarding the formal part of education, one would of course want to take courses directly related to the particular field of STEM of interest (e.g., computer science). But, it is also important to learn and be around other kinds of things like music, art, philosophy, history, and formal linguistics; any of which could help improve one's being an excellent problem solver; and to have a more global perspective on things. The ultimate goal is learning how to think."

Margaret Hamilton

I have always found when I've hired people the combination of the experts and the young kids works best because sometimes the experts can get stuck in a traditional way and the young kids might come out and say, "Why this," right? And I think I've learned along the way from the young kids.

Margaret Hamilton

Abort: to stop or end

Acre: a unit of land area

Algebra: math that uses letters as symbols

Alum / Alumni: a person who attended and graduated from a university or college

Assassinated: to kill a political leader or public figure

Astronaut: a person who travels in space

Avatar: an electronic representation of a person, usually in a video game

BBC: a large broadcasting network based in London, England; stands for British Broadcasting Corporation

Calculus: a type of advanced mathematics

Code: a system of letters, numbers, and symbols that controls the operations of a computer

Cold War: the years of hostile but nonviolent relationships between the former Soviet Union and the U.S. (1947-1990)

Colleagues: co-workers

Command Module: the part of the Apollo ship that carries astronauts back to Earth

Compensating: making up for

Contagious: able to be passed or shared through contact

Cosmonaut: a Soviet Union astronaut

Debris: fragments of something that has been broken or destroyed

Documentary: a factual movie or TV program

Feminism: advocacy of women's rights

Generic: general or overall

Geologist: someone who studies rocks and minerals

Geometry: mathematics that rely on the use of shapes and angles

Keynote Speaker: a person who performs a speech about a primary interest or topic at an assembly; often inspirational and enthusiastic

Lunar Module: the part of the Apollo ship that detaches and lands on the surface of the Moon

Meteorology: the study of weather patterns and systems

Nuisance: problem or pest

Overriding: most important

Philosopher: someone who works to understand and explain reality

Population: the number of people living in a specific place

Portable: able to be moved from one place to another

Quaker: a person who belongs to the Christian group Society of Friends

Revelatory: revealing something that was not previously known

Second-Wave Feminism: feminist movements during the 1960s and '70s, interested with the primary goals of equal pay, workplace equality, and fighting against domestic violence.

Semester: between 15 and 18 weeks of time at some universities and colleges

Simulators: a machine or device that simulates another instrument

Software: the commands that tell a computer what to do

Soviet Union: a communist organization, also known as the USSR; consisted of Armenia, Azerbaijan, Belarus, Estonia, Georgia, Kazakhstan, Kyrgyzstan, Latvia, Lithuania, Moldova, Russia, Tajikistan, Turkmenistan, Ukraine and Uzbekistan.

Sputnik: Russian for "fellow traveler;" This was the first satellite launched by the Soviet Union Space Program.

STEM: abbreviation for Science, Technology, Engineering, and Mathematics

Ton: a unit of measurement, equal to 1,000 kilograms

Vacuum Tubes: a device that controls the flow of electricity within an enclosed space

Wild West: the US Western Frontier associated with chaos and disorder

NASA: National Aeronautics and Space Administration

CM: Command Module

CSDL: Charles Stark Draper Laboratory

FLTs: Funny Little Things

ICSE: International Conference on Software Engineering

JFK: John F. Kennedy

LBJ: Lyndon B. Johnson

LM: Lunar Module

LRV: Lunar Roving Vehicle

MIT: Massachusetts Institute of Technology

RFK: Robert F. Kennedy

SAGE: Semi-Automatic Ground Environment

STEM: Science, Technology, Engineering, Mathematics

WWI: World War One

WWII: World War Two

Tamra Orr is the author of more than 700 nonfiction and educational books for readers of all ages. She graduated from Ball State University with a degree in teaching and English. She lives with her family in the Pacific Northwest. When she isn't writing a book, she is reading one. She believes she has the best job in the world, because she gets to learn something new every day.

1910: Father Kenneth Heafield is born

1914: Mother Ruth Esther Partington is born

August 17th, 1936: Born in Paoli, Indiana

1938: Brother David is born

1941: Sister Kathryn is born

1954: Graduates from Hancock High School

1958: Graduates from Earlham College;
Marries James Cox Hamilton

1959: Daughter Lauren is born;
Begins working at MIT for Project Whirlwind

1961-1963: Works for SAGE

1964: Kenneth Heafield's book is published

1965: Promoted to Team Director in the Draper
Labs

1968: Uses her software to help *Apollo 8*
return back to Earth safely

1969: *Apollo 11* has last minute crisis but is
solved with her software;
Husband opens his own law firm

1976: Leaves NASA and opens her own
company, Higher Order Software

1977: Kenneth Heafield dies

1982: Lauren marries James Cox Chambers;
later, they divorce

1985: Leaves Higher Order Software and
establishes Hamilton Technologies;
Receives Ada Lovelace Award

2003: Receives NASA's Exceptional Space Act Award

2009: Receives the Outstanding Alumni Award from Earlham College

2010: Esther Heafield dies

2014: James Cox Hamilton dies; A photo of Margaret next to the Apollo binders goes viral

2016: Receives the Presidential Medal of Freedom from President Barack Obama

2017: LEGO set modeled after Margaret's famous Apollo photo

2018: Keynote speaker at the International Conference of Software Engineering in Sweden

2000–2020

April 20th, 1910: Halley's Comet visible from Earth

1914 - 1918: World War I

1941-1945: US involvement in World War II

October 4th, 1957: *Sputnik* launched

1958: President Eisenhower signed the public order to create NASA

1961: First American went into space

MIT contacted by NASA to create the computers needed to take astronauts to Moon and back

September 2nd, 1962: President Kennedy gave his famous "Race to Space" Speech

1965: *Gemini 2* launched

December 21st, 1968: *Apollo 8* experiences issues

July 20th, 1969: First Astronauts land on the Moon (*Apollo 11*)

November 14th, 1969: *Apollo 12* launched; Armstrong, Collins, and Aldrin honored with Presidential Medal of Freedom

April 11, 1970: *Apollo 13* launched

January 31st, 1971: *Apollo 14* launched

July 26th, 1971: *Apollo 15* launched, used the lunar roving vehicle (LRV) for the first time

April 16th, 1972: *Apollo 16* launched

December 7th, 1972: *Apollo 17* launched, last of the Apollo missions

May 14th, 1973: Skylab launched

July 11th, 1979: Skylab debris reached Earth

1981: First space shuttle launched

1984: President Ronald Reagan's State of the Union address directed NASA to build an International Space Station [ISS] within 10 years)

1990: Hubble Space Telescope sent into orbit

1997: Mars Pathfinder landed on Mars

1998: First segment of the ISS launched

2000: First crew was sent to live on ISS for several months

2008: European lab and Japanese lab joined ISS

2010 - 2013: SpaceX Dragon became the first commercially built spacecraft to be successfully recovered from orbit

2011: Space shuttle Atlantic completed its flight, the last of the shuttle program

2014 - 2016: SpaceX 14 launched

2017: SpaceX achieved the recovery and reuse of space rockets

2018: NASA's InSight probe landed on Mars

Brown, David. "Q&A: Margaret Hamilton, Who Landed the First Man (and Code) on the Moon." DWB. August 15, 2017.

Cameron, Lori. "What to Know about the Scientist Who Invented the Term 'Software Engineering'". IEEE Computer Society. June 8, 2018.

Chua, Jasmin Malik. "Margaret and the Moon: New Kids' Book Profiles Pioneering Apollo Programmer." Space.com. July 20, 2017.

Cofield, Calla. "'Women of NASA' Lego Set: Q&A with Creator Maia Weinstock." Space.com. March 3, 2017.

Collins, Michael and Edwin E. Aldrin, Jr. "A Yellow Caution Light" from Chapter 11 of Apollo Expeditions to the Moon. NASA.

Creighton, Jolene and Luke Kingma. "Margaret Hamilton: The Untold Story of the Woman Who Took Us to the Moon." Futurism. July 20, 2016.

Doyle, Maria. "The Woman Behind the Software that Took Us to the Moon." PTC. Undated.

Earlham College. "Margaret Hamilton '58—Presidential Medal of Freedom Recipient."

Gee, Sue. "Margaret Hamilton, Apollo, and Beyond." I Programmer. Sept. 5, 2016.

Hamilton, Margaret and William Hackler. "Universal Systems Language: Lessons Learned from Apollo." Computer. December 2008.

Krueger, Pamela. "The Campus Poet Enjoys a Luxury o Time to Spin Thoughts into a Fabric of Words." June 4, 1967. Detroit New Sunday Magazine.

MIT News. "Recalling the 'Giant Leap'". MIT News. July 17 2009.

MacLellan, Lila. "Advice from a Real 'Woman of NASA,' for Kids Who Dream of Working in Science." Quartz. Nov. 3, 2017.

McMillan Robert. "Her Code Got Humans on the Moon—and Invented Software Itself." Wired. Oct. 13, 2015.

NASA. "Margaret Hamilton." NASA Press Release. Sept. 3 2003.

NASA. "Apollo 8: Christmas at the Moon." NASA. Dec. 18, 2014.

Stickgold. Emma. "James Cox Hamilton, at 77: Lawyer was Quiet

Warrior for First Amendment." The Boston Globe. Aug. 31, 2014.

Verne. "Margaret Hamilton, the Engineer Who Took the Apollo to the Moon." Medium. Dec. 25, 2014.

YouTube. "Margaret Hamilton and Grace Hopper Medal of Freedom Ceremony." Nov. 22, 2016. https://www.youtube.com/watch?v=X1PNp_YggAA

YouTube. "Math and Philosophy: Margaret Hamilton MAKERS Moment." July 19, 2017.

YouTube. "Margaret Hamilton Documentary." June 9, 2018.

Weinstock, Maia. "Selecting the Women of NASA." Ideas.lego.com. July 28, 2016.

Edwards, Chris. "All About the Moon Landing." Indianapolis: Blue River Press, 2023.

Adamson, Thomas K. "The First Moon Landing (Graphic History)." Mankato: Capstone Press, 2006

Rocco, John. "How We Got to the Moon: The People, Technology, and Daring of Science Behind Humanity's Greatest Adventure." Crown Books for Young Readers, 2020.

Holt, Nathalia. "Rise of the Rocket Girls: The Women Who Propelled Us, from Missiles to the Moon to Mars." New York: Little Brown and Company, 2016.

Piazza, Domenica Di. "Space Engineer and Scientist Margaret Hamilton (STEM Trailblazer Bios)" LearnerClassroom, 2017.

All About... Series
A series for inquisitive young readers

If you liked this book, you may also enjoy:

All About Amelia Earhart*
All About the Appalachian Trail
All About Barack Obama
All About Benjamin Franklin
All About the Bronte Sisters
All About Frederick Douglass
All About the Grand Canyon
All About the Great Lakes
All About Helen Keller
All About Julia Morgan
All About Madame C.J. Walker
All About Mariano Rivera
All About Marie Curie
All About Martin Luther King, Jr.*
All About the Moon Landing
All About Roberto Clemente
All About Sir Edmund Hillary
All About Stephen Curry
All About Stephen Hawking
All About Steve Wozniak
All About Winston Churchill
All About Yellowstone.

All books are available in print and ebook formats.
Also available as an audiobook!

Teacher guides and puzzles are available at
www.brpressbooks.com/all-about-teachers-guides/